Simple
Pleasures
for
CHRISTMAS

DIMENSIONS
FOR LIVING
NASHVILLE

Simple Pleasures for Christmas

Copyright © 1996 by Dimensions for Living

This book is printed on recycled, acid-free paper.

ISBN 0-687-05590-3

Scripture quotations noted KJV are from the King James Version of the Bible.

Those noted NIV are taken from the Holy Bible: New International Version. Copyright © 1973, 1978, 1984 by the International Bible Society. Used by permission of Zondervan Bible Publishers.

Those noted NRSV are from the New Revised Standard Version Bible, copyright © 1989 by the Division of Christian Education of the National Council of the Churches of Christ in the United States of America, and are used by permission.

96 97 98 99 00 01 02 03 04 05—10 9 8 7 6 5 4 3 2 1

MANUFACTURED IN THE UNITED STATES OF AMERICA

You show me the path of life.
In *your presence there is
fullness of joy;
in your right hand
are pleasures forevermore.*

—Psalm 16:11 NRSV

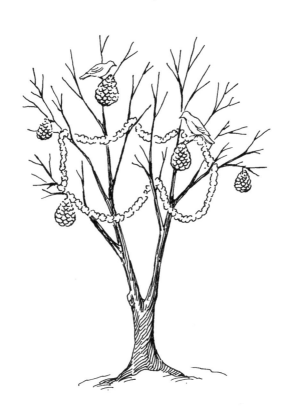

One

*U*se popcorn and pine-cones with peanut butter and birdseed to decorate a tree outside for the birds.

I will say of the LORD, He is my refuge and my fortress: my God; in him will I trust.

—Psalm 91:2 KJV

Two

*T*ake a walk in the woods to collect fresh greenery for Christmas decorations.

Along unfamiliar paths I will guide them; I will turn the darkness into light before them and make the rough places smooth.

—Isaiah 42:16 NIV

Three

*R*ead the Christmas
story out loud with your
family (Luke 2:1-20).

*For this is the covenant that I will make with
the house of Israel after those days, saith the
Lord; I will put my laws into their mind, and
write them in their hearts: and I will be to
them a God, and they shall be to me a people.*

—Hebrews 8:10 KJV

Four

Enclose an index card with a favorite holiday recipe in your Christmas cards.

God loveth a cheerful giver.

—2 Corinthians 9:7 KJV

Five

Take turns caring for the baby Jesus from your crèche in the days before Christmas. On Christmas Eve, gather together to place him in the manger.

You will find a baby wrapped in cloths and lying in a manger.

—Luke 2:12 NIV

Six

Invite a friend who is away from family to join you for Christmas dinner.

Every generous act of giving, with every perfect gift, is from above.

—James 1:17 NRSV

Seven

$\mathcal{S}$hare favorite family
Christmas memories
and stories.

O God, thou hast taught me from my youth:
and hitherto have I declared thy wondrous
works.

—Psalm 71:17 KJV

Eight

Give everyone in the family an instrument (keys, spoons, kazoo) and go caroling in your neighborhood.

Make a joyful noise unto God, all ye lands: Sing forth the honour of his name: make his praise glorious.

—Psalm 66:1-2 KJV

Nine

Re-create one holiday dish that you remember from your childhood.

Nevertheless he left not himself without witness, in that he did good, and gave us rain from heaven, and fruitful seasons, filling our hearts with food and gladness.

—Acts 14:17 KJV

Ten

Go to a Christmas Eve service.

And she brought forth her firstborn son, and wrapped him in swaddling clothes, and laid him in a manger; because there was no room for them in the inn.

—Luke 2:7 KJV

Eleven

𝒲atch your newspaper for the announcement of a Messiah sing-along and join in. You don't have to be able to sing!

For unto us a child is born, unto us a son is given: and the government shall be upon his shoulder: and his name shall be called Wonderful, Counsellor, The mighty God, The everlasting Father, The Prince of Peace.

—Isaiah 9:6 KJV

Twelve

$\mathscr{U}$se paper lunch bags, last year's Christmas cards, a hole punch, and some ribbon to make your own gift bags.

Freely you have received, freely give.

—Matthew 10:8 NIV

Thirteen

*M*ake lots of popcorn and invite another family over to watch a Christmas movie.

Out of the abundance of the heart the mouth speaketh.

—Matthew 12:34 KJV

Fourteen

String popcorn and cranberries for your tree.

Let the heavens rejoice, let the earth be glad; . . .
let the fields be jubilant, and everything in them.
Then all the trees of the forest will sing for joy.

—Psalm 96:11-12 NIV

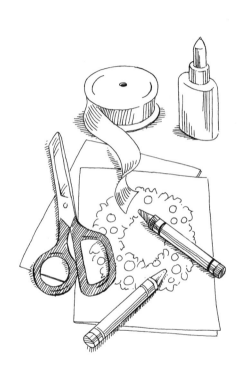

Fifteen

*M*ake your own
Christmas cards.
Everyone in the family
can help.

I thank my God every time I remember you.

—Philippians 1:3 NIV

Sixteen

 _S_ tart a new family
Christmas tradition.
Invite family members to
make suggestions.

Train children in the right way,
and when old, they will not stray.

—Proverbs 22:6 NRSV

Seventeen

*S*et aside one night each week in December as "family night." Choose an activity everyone can enjoy, such as baking, making Christmas cards or gifts, or decorating.

That our sons may be as plants grown up in their youth; that our daughters may be as corner stones, polished after the similitude of a palace.

—Psalm 144:12 KJV

Eighteen

Leave a simple Christmas surprise on the doorstep of a neighbor each night for a week. Then reveal your identity and invite the neighbor or family over for hot chocolate and cookies.

Let every one of us please his neighbour for his good to edification.

—Romans 15:2 KJV

Nineteen

Read your favorite Christmas story to a group of children (family, church family, neighbors, etc.).

Wherefore comfort yourselves together, and edify one another, even as also ye do.

—1 Thessalonians 5:11 KJV

BABYSITTING
COUPON

GOOD FOR:

TWO SATURDAY
NIGHTS

Twenty

Volunteer to baby-sit for friends or family during the holidays—or give a baby-sitting coupon to someone as a Christmas gift.

Then were there brought unto him little children, that he should put his hands on them, and pray.

—Matthew 19:13 KJV

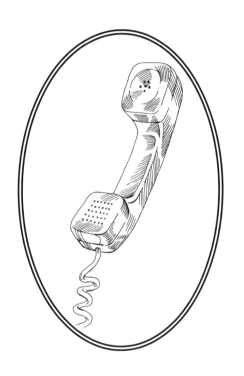

Twenty-one

Call an old friend you haven't stayed in touch with to say, "Merry Christmas!"

And when they had seen it, they made known abroad the saying which was told them concerning this child.

—Luke 2:17 KJV

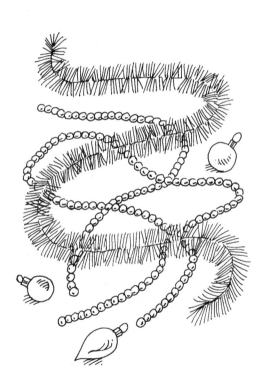

Twenty-two

Help a person who is homebound decorate for Christmas.

Praise be to the God and Father of our Lord Jesus Christ, the Father of compassion and the God of all comfort, who comforts us in all our troubles, so that we can comfort those in any trouble with the comfort we ourselves have received from God.

—2 Corinthians 1:3-4 NIV

TO:

FROM:

Twenty-three

Make gift tags from old Christmas cards.

*Being confident of this very thing, that he
which hath begun a good work in you will
perform it until the day of Jesus Christ.*

—Philippians 1:6 KJV

Twenty-four

*A*dopt a nursing home resident. Find out special days like birthdays, and plan to visit at least six times in the coming year.

Just as you excel in everything—in faith, in speech, in knowledge, in complete earnestness and in your love for us—see that you also excel in this grace of giving.

—2 Corinthians 8:7 NIV

Twenty-five

Begin a tradition of buying each family member a dated ornament, or make a simple ornament for each person and date it.

Let love and faithfulness never leave you;
bind them around your neck,
write them on the tablet of your heart.

—Proverbs 3:3 NIV

Twenty-six

Buy a simple Advent wreath and candles. Pick a time each day to light the candle(s) together. Read a devotion, sing a carol, or say a prayer.

Let us walk in the light of the LORD.

—Isaiah 2:5 KJV

Twenty-seven

Make your own Christmas countdown calendar. In the square for each day in December, write something simple that family members can do to show their love for others.

Love your neighbor as yourself.

—Matthew 22:39 NIV

Twenty-eight

Turn off all the lights except those on the Christmas tree. Listen to Christmas music and drink spiced tea.

And suddenly there was with the angel a multitude of the heavenly host praising God, and saying,
Glory to God in the highest, and on earth peace, good will toward men.

—Luke 2:13-14 KJV

Twenty-nine

Go "window shopping" in a bookstore. Look through all the new Christmas books and choose one.

But Mary treasured all these words and pondered them in her heart.

—Luke 2:19 NRSV

Thirty

$\mathcal{G}$et dressed up and walk through the public areas of a large hotel, admiring the decorations. Perhaps you can have tea and listen to live music at no charge.

And the Word was made flesh, and dwelt among us, (and we beheld his glory, the glory as of the only begotten of the Father,) full of grace and truth.

—John 1:14 KJV